Looking at Small Mammals

Insect Eaters

Sally Morgan

Chrysalis Children's Books

First published in the UK in 2004
⑥ Chrysalis Children's Books
An imprint of Chrysalis Books Group PLC,
The Chrysalis Building, Bramley Road,
London W10 6SP

Editorial Manager: Joyce Bentley
Series editor: Debbie Foy
Editors: Clare Lewis, Joseph Fullman
Designer: Wladek Szechter
Picture researcher: Sally Morgan
Illustrations: Woody

ISBN 1 844458 102 0

Printed in China

10 9 8 7 6 5 4 3 2 1

British Library Cataloguing in Publication
Data for this book is available from the
British Library.

Picture acknowledgements:
Corbis: 7T, 11B, Michael and Patricia Fogden.
Ecoscene: 12 Ian Beames, 26 Michael Gore,
9TL, 22 Chinch Gryniewicz, 26/27B Dennis
Johnson, 16 Kevin King, 4 Martin Lillicrap,
1C, 7B, 9B, 17B, 18 Papilio/Steve Austin, 5T
Papilio/William Dunn, 27 Papilio/Paul
Franklin, 11T, 20, 24 Papilio/Jamie Harron,
21T Papilio/Robert Pickett, 21B Judyth Platt,
5B, 6, 9TR, 10, 13T, 13B, 14, 15B, 17T, 19, 32
Robin Redfern. Front cover: TCL
Papilio/William Dunn, R Martin Lillicrap,
TCR, CL, CR, B Robin Redfern. Back cover:
TCL Papilio/ William Dunn, TR Martin
Lillicrap, TCR Robin Redfern.
Frank Lane Picture Agency: 23 E Schuiling.
NHPA: 25 Daniel Heuclin.
Still Pictures: 15T Roland Seitre.

Contents

What are insect eaters?

Hedgehogs, shrews and moles are all insect eaters. Insect eaters belong to a group of animals called **mammals**.

A hedgehog's back is covered in prickly hairs.

Moles use their large front paws to dig through the soil.

Most mammals have four legs and are covered in hair. They give birth to live young. Young mammals feed on their mother's milk for the first weeks of their lives.

Shrews have an excellent sense of smell.

The insect eater family

Insect eaters have a face with small eyes and ears and a long narrow **snout**. Their legs are short and they have five toes on each of their feet.

This pygmy shrew is pushing its nose into a crack to find food.

The golden mole lives in sandy deserts.

The proper name for the group of mammals to which the insect eaters belong is *Insectivora*.

Shrews run quickly on their four short legs.

Where do insect eaters live?

Insect eaters are found all over the world apart from Australia and New Zealand. They are only found in parts of South America.

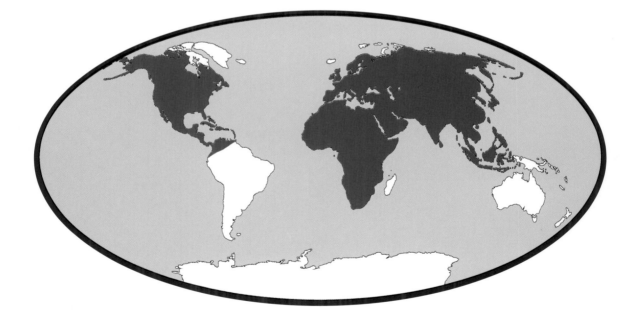

The areas shaded in pink on this map of the world show where insect eaters live.

The water shrew lives by ponds, lakes and rivers.

Insect eaters live in

rainforests, woodlands,

grasslands and even in deserts.

Hedgehogs are found in city streets and gardens as well as in woodlands and fields.

What do insect eaters eat?

Insect eaters eat insects
but they also eat lots
of other types
of food, too.

This shrew has found an insect hidden under the bark.

A hedgehog has found a fat worm in the ground.

They like to eat worms, slugs and snails. Water shrews feed on frogs, fish and crabs. The hedgehog may eat bird's eggs and even kill chickens. Shrews

and solendons have a **poisonous** bite. The **poison** kills their **prey**.

This golden mole is eating a large desert locust.

11

Finding food

Insect eaters use their senses to find food, especially their sense of smell and hearing. The hedgehog finds food using its long snout and by digging with its clawed feet.

Hedgehogs sniff in the undergrowth to find food.

Shrews have tiny eyes and rely on their ears and noses to find food. They have many **whiskers** on their snout. Whiskers are **sensitive** to touch and they provide information about the animal's surroundings.

A shrew stands on its back feet to pick up smells in the air.

Getting around

Most insect eaters run along the forest floor.

Shrews can climb up trees and shrubs. The water

shrew, otter shrew and some tenrecs can swim.

The water shrew can swim across streams and ponds.

Desmans are excellent swimmers. They find nearly all of their food in water.

These swimmers have a slender body and a flattened head. This allows their ears, eyes and nostrils to stick up above the surface of the water while their body remains under the water. Some have **webbed** toes that help them to swim.

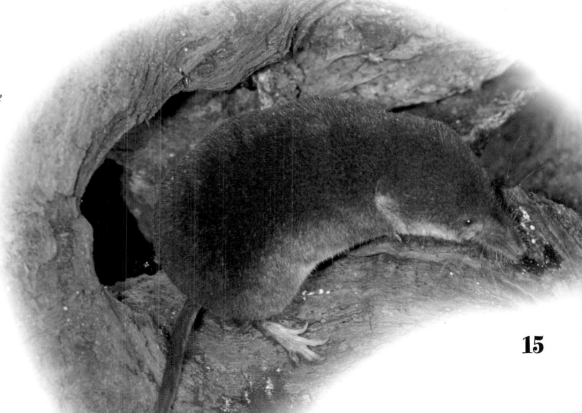

Shrews are nimble animals that can climb trees and run along walls.

15

Living underground

Some insect eaters, such as moles and some tenrecs, live underground in **tunnels**. The mole digs a network of tunnels.

Moles have burrowed in this lawn and made several molehills.

A mole is burrowing its way through the soil to the surface, pushing hard with its large front paws.

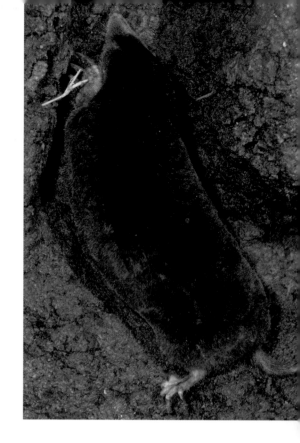

Moles find most of their food in their tunnels as insects and other animals drop in from the surrounding soil. Moles' hands are shaped for digging. They are like big **paddles** with long claws. They are ideal for pushing soil.

A mole has found a worm as it burrowed through the soil.

Surviving the cold

Insect eaters are small animals who have to eat lots of food to stay warm. For example, shrews have to eat all day. If they go without food they die.

This shrew is eating a large slug that it has found in the undergrowth.

Hedgehogs spend the winter asleep under a pile of leaves.

Each day a shrew has to eat almost its own body weight in food to stay alive. Shrews make their nests in **burrows** and under logs where they can stay warm. Hedgehogs avoid cold weather by **hibernating**. In late autumn, they creep into a warm place, curl up and go into a deep sleep. They wake up in spring when it is warmer.

Spiny skin

The hedgehog is best known for the **spines** that cover its body. The spines are long and face backwards.

A hedgehog licks its spines. Nobody is sure why they do this, but perhaps it is to keep them clean.

The hedgehog
also has hairs that
lie between the spines.
When a hedgehog is
threatened by a **predator**,
it tucks its head in and rolls
into a ball so that all the sharp
spines are pointing outwards.

The hedgehog protects itself by rolling up into a tight ball and tucking its head under its body.

Nothing will try to eat it! Some tenrecs
have spines and they can roll into a ball, too.

Baby insect eaters

Most insect eaters build a nest in a warm, dry place. They give birth to a **litter** of small babies. Their babies are pink because they do not have any fur.

These newborn baby hedgehogs have a small number of white spines. They grow more spines quickly.

Their eyes are closed at first. They feed on their mother's milk. Hedgehogs and tenrecs live for up to eight years, but shrews only live between 12 and 18 months.

Tenrecs can produce large litters of up to 32 babies.

Growing up fast

Young insect eaters have to grow up quickly.

Their eyes open and they start to grow fur.

Soon they leave their nest to explore outside.

Within a month or so, they will be old enough

to live on their own.

These young hedgehogs are ready to live on their own.

Young shrews form a line behind their mother when they leave their nest.

Shrews grow very quickly. When they first leave the nest, baby shrews form a line, each baby shrew gripping the back of the one in front, with their mother leading them. Their mother guides them around. This is called a caravan.

Anteaters use their claws to rip open termite nests. They use their long snout to reach for the termites.

Other insect eaters

Insect eaters are not the only mammals that eat insects. Bats, anteaters, pangolins and armadillos all eat insects. Bats catch flying insects such as moths.

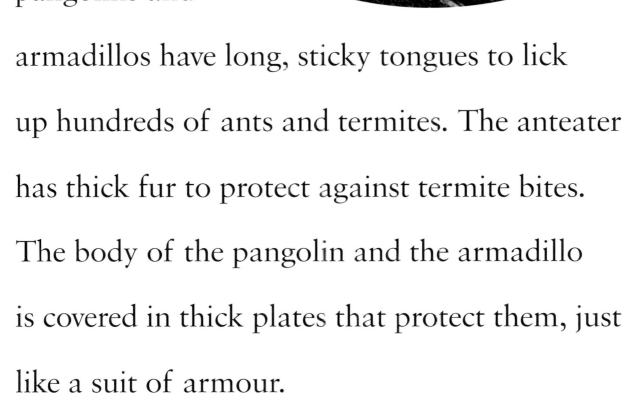

The armadillo uses its sense of smell to find insects on the forest floor.

Anteaters, pangolins and armadillos have long, sticky tongues to lick up hundreds of ants and termites. The anteater has thick fur to protect against termite bites. The body of the pangolin and the armadillo is covered in thick plates that protect them, just like a suit of armour.

Pangolins sleep in burrows during the day, coming out at night to feed.

27

Investigate!

Spiny protection

Take a small rectangular piece of foam and 30 cocktail sticks. Push one end of a cocktail stick into the foam, so that the stick lies at an angle. Push all the other sticks into the foam in the same way. Imagine this is your hedgehog. Now pretend the hedgehog is rolling into a ball by bending the foam into a ball shape. All the 'spines' should stick out. This is how spiny insect eaters, such as hedgehogs and some tenrecs, protect themselves from danger.

Push each cocktail stick into the foam and watch what happens when you roll the foam into a ball.

Insect eaters in the garden

Many people have hedgehogs in their garden. You can attract hedgehogs by putting food out for them. They like to eat dog or cat food. People are not so pleased to have moles in their garden! Moles leave molehills on the lawn. Find some molehills. How far apart are they? Are the molehills in a line? If you look carefully you may find the entrance to the tunnel. Take a look but be careful not to disturb the tunnel.

Hedgehogs may eat the food you put out during the night when it is quiet in the garden.

Finding out more

You can learn more about insect eaters by reading about them in books or searching for information about them on the Internet.

New molehills can appear in the lawn overnight.

Insect eater facts

✓ Moles eat up to 50g of worms a day. During the winter months they store worms, with their heads bitten off, near their nest.

✓ The Eurasian shrew must eat up to 80 percent of its body weight each day just to stay alive!

✓ The Etruscan or pygmy white-toothed shrew is the smallest mammal. It is so small that it can sit in a teaspoon.

✓ The star-nosed mole is named after its strange nose, which ends in 22 tentacles or 'rays'. The mole uses its nose to sniff and feel for prey in water.

These silhouettes show the size of a tencrec, a desman and a hedgehog compared with the size a human foot.

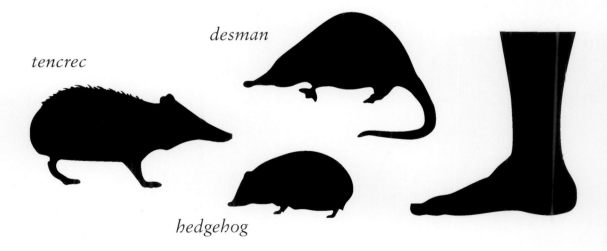

desman

tencrec

hedgehog

Glossary

burrow A hole in the ground dug by an animal.

hibernate To go into a deep sleep to survive cold weather.

litter The young of an animal born at the same time, to the same mother.

mammal An animal that feeds their young milk and is usually covered in fur.

paddle A short, broad spoon-shaped oar.

poison A harmful substance.

poisonous Something that contains poison.

predator An animal that hunts other animals.

prey An animal that is hunted by other animals.

sensitive Able to detect the slightest touch.

snout A long nose.

spine A special hair that is long, thick and pointed.

tunnel An underground passage.

webbed A flap of skin between the toes that helps an animal to swim.

whisker Stiff hairs found around the mouth and nose of a mammal.

Index